T0169372

Soul of Marrakesh

A GUIDE TO 30 EXCEPTIONAL EXPERIENCES

WRITTEN BY FABRICE NADJARI AND ZOHAR BENJELLOUN
PHOTOS BY ABDELAALI AIT KARROUM
ILLUSTRATED BY ANNAELLE MYRIAM CHAAIB

JONGLEZ PUBLISHING

Travel guides

'THERE ARE FEW CITIES IN
THE WORLD THAT BEWITCH YOU
AS POWERFULLY AND WITH THE
SAME MAGIC AS MARRAKESH.
THERE ARE FEW CITIES AND FEW
COUNTRIES THAT GIVE SO MUCH.'

PIERRE BERGÉ

How can you capture the soul of Marrakesh?

For the two of us – both in love with Morocco and both journeying between Marrakesh and our respective countries of exile – this is at once one of the most intriguing and difficult questions. We've scoured the nooks and crannies of this captivating city in order to distil the most striking and unexpected experiences. Out of the more than 1,000 places and experiences we tested, we selected just 30.

Yves St Laurent's private library, the best orange juice in the legendary Jamaa el-Fna square, the most beautiful riads and the best restaurants far from the tourist crowds, the search of the perfect carpet, a night in a tent in the desert, a secret museum where everything is for sale …

Far from the well-trodden paths of Marrakesh, we invite you to immerse yourself in the more intimate side of this extraordinary city, discover its best-kept secrets and enjoy the most offbeat, intense experiences … In the words of the Spanish writer and poet Juan Goytisolo, 'If you let yourself fall under the spell of Marrakesh, everywhere else in the world will seem boring.'

Rihlat saeida
    Bon voyage !

WHAT YOU WON'T FIND
IN THIS GUIDE

- the best place to ride a camel
- all-inclusive hotels
- how to pour mint tea
- tips for haggling
- a detailed map of the Medina

WHAT YOU WILL FIND
IN THIS GUIDE

- the phone number of the best second-hand dealer in Marrakesh
- a playlist of the best Moroccan sounds
- local artists' best-loved greasy spoons
- the city's most beautiful hidden corners and most charming riads
- the locals' favourite spots in the Medina
- the best Arabica coffee ever
- the art of making perfume

SYMBOLS USED IN
'SOUL OF MARRAKESH'

100–300
Moroccan
dirhams

300–500
Moroccan
dirhams

500–2,000
Moroccan
dirhams

You need a car
to get here

Reservation
recommended

Cash
only

Ask a local!

Opening times often vary,
so we recommend checking them directly
on the website of the place you plan to visit.

30 EXPERIENCES

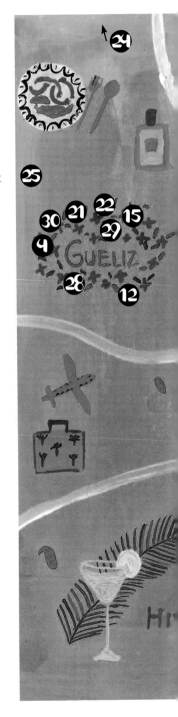

OUED
TENSIF

BAB
EL
KHEMIS

JARDIN
MAJORELLE

PALMERAIE

MEDINA

ATLAS

SOUK

KOUTOUBIA

JAGE

TAXI

11

THE MOST
BEAUTIFUL RIADS

Marrakesh has countless charming riads. But don't worry, you won't need to spend hours online to find that rare gem: we've compiled a selection of the best addresses for you.

> Ksar Char-Bagh: the old Andalusian Palace

Ksar Char-Bagh is a small private palace set in the heart of Marrakesh's beautiful Palmeraie. From the large Moorish patio, you can admire the fountains and the citrus and olive groves that stretch as far as the eye can see in the hotel's vast park. After dark, immerse yourself in the books in the art library or head to the old smoking lounge, which encourages visitors to share their secrets. A place brimming with history, where every passing day is a journey in itself.

KSAR CHAR-BAGH
DJNAN ABIAD,
LA PALMERAIE B.P. 12478

+212 5243-29244

info@ksarcharbagh.fr
conciergerie@ksarcharbagh.fr
ksarcharbagh.fr

© ICOR DEMBA

> Riad El Fenn: an oasis in the Medina

Vanessa and Howell Branson became hoteliers somewhat by accident, opening El Fenn in 2004 after falling in love with it at first sight. Divided into several riads, El Fenn is considered one of the city's most beautiful hotels, its every detail a perfect combination of luxury and authenticity. The decor, colours, fabrics and furnishings are constantly revamped to provide a new experience each time you visit. Make sure to check out the sumptuous rooftop, a perfect perch from which to gaze out over the Medina.

RIAD EL FENN
DERB MOULAY ABDELLAH BEN HEZZIAN,
BAB EL KSOUR

+212 5 24 44 12 20

contact@el-fenn.com
el-fenn.com

> Jnane Tamsna: the secret garden in Palmeraie

The Jnane Tamsna riad combines elegant interior design by Meryanne Loum-Martin (as chic here as in her hotel) with the serenity of a garden under the care of her botanist husband, Gary Martin. A fusion of architecture and nature that makes this boutique hotel one of a kind – friendly yet mysterious, just like its creators.

 **JNANE TAMSNA, DOUAR ABIAD
LA PALMERAIE**

| +212 5 24 32 84 84 | requests@jnanetamsna.com
jnanetamsna.com |

© JNANE TAMSNA

© JNANE TAMSNA

© TARABEL MARRAKECH

> Riad de Tarabel: the villa suspended in time ▲

Time seems to have stood still at Riad de Tarabel, with its tree-lined patios, intimate atmosphere and birds of paradise. A former colonial residence, this house for aesthetes evokes refinement and calm in a decor that subtly blends vestiges of Arab-Andalusian architecture with a Second Empire style. A delicious sense of idleness, like in the golden age of the Red City. And superb cooking, exclusively for guests.

 RIAD DE TARABEL
DERB SRAGHNA, QUARTIER DAR EL BACHA
MARRAKECH MÉDINA

+212 5 24 39 17 06

contact@tarabelmarrakech.com
tarabelmarrakech.com

> Riad Farnatchi: 'the original'

Since 2004, Riad Farnatchi has grown from a small B&B to a luxurious five-star hotel on a human scale. It features a dozen rooms (each more sumptuous than the next), a superlative spa and one of the city's most sought-after restaurants. Here, attention to detail is a philosophy and ensuring guests' well-being a way of life.

LE FARNATCHI
DERB EL FARNATCHI,
RUE SOUK EL FASSIS QUA'AT BEN AHID

+212 5 24 38 49 10
+212 5 24 38 49 12

info@lefarnatchi.com
riadfarnatchi.com

> Casa Gyla: the romantic villa

In the middle of the golden triangle of Marrakesh's Palmeraie lies the mysterious Casa Gyla, an Arab-Andalusian villa built by the architect Jacqueline Foissac and her lover, the Spanish painter Alejandro Reino. In the shade of cypress trees, the house nestles in a lush garden dotted with bougainvillea, century-old olive trees and rosebushes that spread their intoxicating perfume along the paths of the park.

CASA GYLA
VILLA HAROUCHI
ROUTE DES JARDINS DE LA PALMERAIE

+212 707-785604

> Le Jardin Djahane: the hidden secret of the Medina

This luxurious traditional 18th-century riad is named after Djahane, the revered lover of Persian poet Omar Khayyam. Five suites and four heavenly gardens invite you to enjoy a divine respite in the Bab Aylen district in the heart of the old Medina. A true love nest, where you can relax surrounded by the palm trees, turtles and chameleons that have made this place their own.

LE JARDIN DJAHANE
32 DERB CAID RASSOU

+212 648508169

lejardindjahane@gmail.com
lejardindjahane.com

> Riad Kniza: the Bouskri family jewel

In the heart of the old city, a few blocks from Jemaa el Fnaa square, stands Riad Kniza, a superb 18th-century building that has been owned by the Bouskri family for over 200 years. The current owner, Mohammed Bouskri – who is a famous antique dealer in the city – has decorated his riad with all the treasures of Morocco. In this fabulous setting, you're sure to appreciate the peace and quiet that reign in this little oasis of luxury.

RIAD KNIZA
34 DERB L'HOTEL,
BAB DOUKALA

+212 5 24 37 69 42

riadkniza.com

> Riad Malika: the riad with flair

In the heart of one of the most beautiful districts of the Medina, home to antique dealers and the Dar el Bacha Palace, lies Riad Malika. In an oasis of pink bougainvillea and orange trees, this unusual bourgeois home holds many surprises, starting with its artwork and furniture, which reveal a pronounced penchant for the great designers of the 20th century.

RIAD MALIKA
29 ARSET AOUZAL

	+212 5 24 38 54 51	contact@riadmalika.com riadmalika.com

© DOMAINE MALIKA

AN UNLIKELY
FLEA MARKET

A former livestock souk, Bab el Khemis has turned into a huge flea market over the years. Amidst a sea of bric-a-brac, bargain hunters will find everything that Marrakesh has to offer in terms of crafts. At one street corner, you'll even find second-hand dealers specialising in the sale of magnificent antique wooden doors, often salvaged from crumbling old palaces. Needless to say, everything is organised so that you can take it all home with you.

The hustle and bustle is at its height on Thursdays, which are all about new arrivals and bargains. Follow the same customs as at every other market in Marrakesh: make sure to linger, rummage and haggle.

📍 **BAB EL KHEMIS**

SAT-THU: 10am / 7pm

© KASIA GATKOWSKA

23

RENDEZVOUS WITH
MOROCCAN POP ART

> Riad Yima: the temple of Moroccan pop art

It's all there: the colours, posing visitors and crème de la kitsch. Tucked away behind the Place des Épices (Square of the Spice Sellers), Riad Yima is a reflection of its creator: extravagant and multicultural. Renovated in 2006 by the artist Hassan Hajjaj, who needs no introduction, this traditional old house, which still calls itself a riad even though it no longer serves as a guest house, has become a sanctuary of Moroccan–Warholian pop art.

Almost everything here is for sale. You can wander around the house, from art gallery to tea room, browse in the shop or take a Berber cooking class with the in-house cordon bleu. A must-see, right in the city centre.

 TEASHOP RIAD YIMA
52 DERB AARJANE RAHBA LAKDIMA MEDINA

| DAILY: 9am / 6:30pm | +212 5 24 39 19 87 | riadyima@yahoo.co.uk |
| | | contact@riadyima.com |

> Jajjah: all the flavours of Marrakesh pop culture

If you like artist Hassan Hajjaj's Riad Yima, this is the place for you. The Moroccan pop art pioneer has just opened a new space that's as colourfully hybrid as his first one in the industrial district of Sidi Ghanem.

There's a tea room with his brand of drinks, Jajjah, a restaurant that pays tribute to the dishes of his childhood and, needless to say, an exhibition space where you can discover his latest creations.

JAJJAH
141 RAHBA LAKDIMA, PLACE DES ÉPICES, MÉDINA

| TUE-SUN: 10am / 6pm | +212 6 73 46 02 09 |

THE SLOW-FASHION
PRODIGY

Born in Jerusalem, the designer Artsi Ifrach settled in Morocco after wandering between Tel Aviv, Paris and Amsterdam. A professional classical dancer, this Marrakshi-at-heart came to fashion later in life. He is passionate about art, history and materials, and his brand ARTC reflects his multiculturalism: rich, colourful and eclectic. The slow pace of Marrakesh has rubbed off on his practice, turning him into a follower of 'slow fashion'. His creations are made of vintage fabrics found in markets around the world, and his inspirations are as far-ranging as his travel diaries. Make sure to visit his showroom in the Guéliz district: Artsi will be there to welcome you.

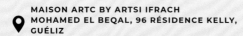

MAISON ARTC BY ARTSI IFRACH
MOHAMED EL BEQAL, 96 RÉSIDENCE KELLY,
GUÉLIZ

DAILY: 11am / 6pm

Make an appointment on
+212 6 65 03 55 10

info@maisonartc.com
maisonartc.com

05

A GARDEN
AS A SURREALIST
WORK OF ART

Here's an unusual garden that will be a hit on your Instagram page! A maze of prickly plants interspersed with surrealist sculptures, this botanical scene is the brainchild of the Austrian artist André Heller. Just 30 minutes from Marrakesh, this African Garden of Eden is a true green gem, the ideal destination for an afternoon of fresh air.

After wandering around, stop for a snack at the Paul Bowles café while admiring the view of the Atlas Mountains.

ANIMA
DOUAR SBITI, ROUTE D'OURIKA

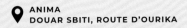

DAILY: 9am / 6pm	+212 5 24 48 20 22 info@anima-garden.com anima-garden.com	Admission from 6€ (free shuttle from Marrakesh included in the price of the ticket)

© ANIMA

AN ENIGMATIC LIBRARY
OPEN BY APPOINTMENT ONLY

Yves Saint Laurent has left a tremendous legacy in Marrakesh. In addition to the Majorelle Garden, the sumptuous Villa Oasis and an incredible art collection, the French couturier left behind an enigmatic research library housed inside the Yves Saint Laurent Museum. Packed with rare books, it's open (by appointment only) to anyone who can justify a serious interest in the archives. While many of the books are about Morocco, the library also holds special collections on the legendary designer and on fashion. In preparation for your visit, have a look at the online catalogue.

BIBLIOTHÈQUE DU MUSÉE YVES SAINT LAURENT
RUE YVES ST LAURENT

| WED–SUN: 9am / 6pm | +212 5242-98686 | museeyslmarrakech.com/fr/bibliotheque |

STORYTELLING TIME
AT LE CAFÉ CLOCK

Some of the stories you'll hear here are as old as the world. They've been passed down through the ages, from mouth to mouth, to Café Clock, whose storytellers, in turn, will share them with you. Every Monday and Thursday at 7pm, come and immerse yourself in Moroccan folklore as you listen to these traditional fables in English or Darija. If you're lucky, you'll catch Hajj Ahmed Ezzarghani, the master storyteller, who will transport you to another space-time entirely.

LE CAFÉ CLOCK
224 DERB CHTOUKA, KASBAH

DAILY: 9am / 10pm	+212 5243-78367	info@cafeclock.com
Storytelling evening on		cafeclock.com/visions-stories
Monday and Thursday at 7pm		

TIFINAGH
OR THE BEAUTY OF
THE BERBER ALPHABET

Strange geometric symbols engraved in stone nearly 3,000 years ago are the oldest traces of what is now called the Tifinagh alphabet, whose origins remain as mysterious as its almost extraterrestrial aesthetic. After falling into disuse and then being reintroduced 30 years ago, this alphabet is still used to write Tamazight, the language spoken by Berber populations in North Africa.

The Tuareg, 'the blue men of the Sahara', are currently the only Berber-speaking people to actively use the Tifinagh script, though many Moroccans speak Tamazight. In fact, over a quarter of the kingdom's population uses one of the country's three main Berber dialects (Tarifit, Tamazight and Tachelhit). But across North Africa, where Berbers have lived for centuries and still live today, many other languages are spoken, including Nafusi, Siwi and Zenaga. Moroccan multiculturalism is a reflection of these ancient populations: tenacious and mixed.

#08

BLACK SOAP, SCRUBBING **AND RECONNECTING WITH YOURSELF**

An age-old institution and a Middle Eastern beauty ritual, going to the hammam is a not-to-be-missed experience in Marrakesh. To shed your old skin, treat yourself to an hour or more of soaping down, scrubbing and massage in this haven of relaxation. An excellent way to take a breather from your exploration of the bustling Moroccan city.

> La Sultana Spa: the hammam of kings

This spa, located in Marrakesh's smallest five-star hotel, La Sultana, could be straight out of a palace in *The Arabian Nights*. In this architectural gem, the washing rituals take place around an antique pool made of pink marble. A luxurious space designed to satisfy the most demanding of customers.

m.lasultanahotels.com

> Les Bains de Marrakech: the most local hammam

Recently renovated, this Marrakesh institution retains the purely traditional character of an authentic Middle Eastern hammam. Enjoy a salt crystal or sugar scrub, rhassoul ritual or scented bath.

lesbainsdemarrakech.com

> Hammam de la Rose: the Medina hammam

Washing with black soap, scrubbing with spices and moisturising your skin with essential oils … Hamman de la Rose offers a range of revitalising treatments in the heart of the Medina. A chance to take a well-deserved break without leaving the city centre.

hammamdelarose.com

> Les Bains de Tarabel: lose track of time

Nowhere have the traditional Maghreb beauty secrets been better kept than at Les Bains de Tarabel. Next to the hotel of the same name, this cosy hammam offers a wonderful moment of relaxation seemingly outside the stream of time. We recommend the foot bath with sea salts and bitter orange essence.

lesbainsdetarabel.com

> Royal Mansour: the ultimate hammam experience

Owned by the King of Morocco, the Royal Mansour is one of the most exclusive places in Marrakesh. Inside, you'll discover a spectacular hammam and custom-made treatments so you can try out the Red City's age-old rituals for yourself.

royalmansour.com

#09

PLAY IT
LIKE PRINCE

Aya's, a small made-to-measure clothing boutique, has been located on a quiet street in the Medina since 2001. Its founder, Nawal el Hariti, has built an international reputation – Prince himself was one of her customers ...

If you have something specific in mind, you've come to the right place. After a brainstorming session, head to the souk to buy fabric and ornaments, then back to the studio for fittings and lunch with the designer. Then wait a few days and, voilà, your divine outfit awaits you!

 **SHOP AYA'S MARRAKESH**

+212 6 61 46 29 16   ayasmarrakech.com
info@ayasmarrakech.com

THE RESTAURANT
FOR LARGE
GATHERINGS

Dar Yacout, one of the cult restaurants in the Medina, is not to be missed. Both its decor and its menu offer an excellent introduction to Moroccan culture. Renowned for its traditional dishes, this dinner-only institution has made a name for itself with a few local specialities: an almond chicken to die for and wonderful cinnamon oranges. Before you sit down to dinner, head up to the terrace to admire a view of the Koutoubia mosque against the setting sun.

 DAR YACOUT
79 DERB SIDI AHMED SOUSSI,
BAB DOUKKALA

+212 5 24 38 29 29
+212 5 24 38 29 00

yacout@menara.ma
daryacout.com

© DAR YACOUT

FEEL LIKE A PASHA
WHILE SIPPING
A MOCHA

Marrakesh, 1910. Colette, Maurice Ravel, Josephine Baker and Winston Churchill meet for an Arabic coffee at the Dar el Bacha Palace – 'the pasha's house'. Over a century later, this historic building, now restored and known as the Musée des Confluences, still has its precious lounge nestled inside an inner courtyard. You can choose your 100% Arabica coffee by continent, bean type and time of day.

© BACHA COFFE MARRAKECH - DAR EL BACHA, MUSÉE DES CONFLUENCES

BACHA COFFEE MARRAKECH
ROUTE SIDI ABDELAZIZ

TUE–SUN: 10am / 6pm | +212 5 24 38 12 93

ART WALK
IN MARRAKESH

As Marrakesh begins to make a name for itself in the international art market, galleries are proliferating in the city centre, especially in the trendy Guéliz district. Here's a little cultural jaunt through the area that we've put together for you.

> Voice Gallery

Located on the outskirts of the city in the industrial zone of Sidi Ghanem, Voice Gallery has become one of the city's most renowned art galleries. Founded by Rocco Orlacchio in 2011, shortly after the start of the Arab Spring, the venue only exhibits one artist at a time, regardless of the medium used, just as long as the work questions, challenges and resonates.

VOICE GALLERY
RUE SALAH EDDINE AL AYOUBI

| TUE–SAT: 10am / 6pm | +212 658482800 | info@voicegallery.net voicegallery.net |

© GALERIE TINDOUF

> Tindouf Gallery

Established in 2007, Galerie Tindouf has built a reputation in the field of contemporary and fine arts. Its unique pieces by renowned artisans and artists are carefully selected by curator Boubker Temli, who can also tell you the story behind them.

TINDOUF GALLERY
22 BOULEVARD MOHAMMED VI

| MON-SAT: 10am / 1pm 3:30pm / 8pm | +212 5244 30908 | galerietindouf.com |

> Galerie 127

Galerie 127, devoted exclusively to contemporary Moroccan photography, opened its doors in 2006. The first and only gallery of its kind in Morocco, it has already made a name for itself beyond the Mediterranean. A must-see for photography lovers.

GALERIE 127
127 AVENUE MOHAMED V, GUÉLIZ

THU–SAT: 3pm / 6pm or by appointment	+212 5 24 43 26 67

> Comptoir des Mines Gallery

Nestled in a 1930s Art Deco building, the Comptoir des Mines is part of Marrakesh's historical and cultural heritage. Transformed into an art centre, it has become the point of reference for the new Moroccan art scene. Don't miss it – both the works and the building are worth a visit.

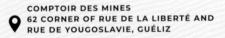

COMPTOIR DES MINES
62 CORNER OF RUE DE LA LIBERTÉ AND RUE DE YOUGOSLAVIE, GUÉLIZ

+212 6 73 25 76 91	comptoirdesminesgalerie.com

© COMPTOIR DES MINES

© DAVID BLOCH GALLERY

> David Bloch Gallery

Initially based in Casablanca, Parisian David Bloch opened this very New York-style gallery in Marrakesh in 2010. Now one of the most exclusive in Guéliz, its ultra-modern display window unabashedly attracts attention. As for its exhibitions, they've been known to sometimes spill out onto the street …

DAVID BLOCH GALLERY
8 BIS RUE DES VIEUX MARRAKCHIS

TUE–SUN: 11am / 6pm	+212 5 24 45 75 95	instagram.com/davidblochgallery

> Al Maqam

Located in Tahanaout, about 30 km from Marrakesh, this artists' residence, created by the painter Mohamed Mourabiti, is a unique and extremely versatile place. A meeting point for local creatives, Al Maqam is also a gallery, literary café and restaurant, lost in a sea of olive trees.

AL MAQAM
EL MGASSEM, MARRAKECH TENSIFT AL HAOUZ,
42302 TAHANNAOUT

	+212 5244-84002	

IN SEARCH OF
THE PERFECT CARPET

Talking about Moroccan artisanship without mentioning carpets is inconceivable. In Marrakesh, you'll find hundreds of shops selling more or less authentic ones. We recommend a trip to the showrooms of Soufiane and Ismaïl Zarib, two brothers who have rugs in their blood, as it were. Foregoing shop windows and displays, their business runs by word of mouth. Inside, you'll find hundreds of carpets from the Beni Ourain, Taznakht and Boujad regions displayed in modern salons that will make you want to redo your interior. You're bound to find the rug of your dreams here.

SHOWROOM 16
16 RUE RIAD LAÂROUSS
DAR EL BACHA

BOUTIQUE ZARIB
RUE HOUDDOUD
MAJORELLE

+212 6 15 28 56 90
+212 6 61 85 34 87

soufiane-zarib.com

- **Beni Ourain:** knotted wool carpet. Usually white and black, the patterns on these rugs are rather simple and presented graphically.

- **Azilal:** knotted wool carpet. Visually busier, these rugs can be very colourful or black and white.

- **Boujad:** highly original decorative item that should be considered a work of art. Some models take months to complete.

- **Boucherouite:** patchwork rug made of recycled materials such as fabric and scraps of clothing.

- **Beni Mguild:** made in the Middle Atlas Mountains, these carpets were originally designed for use in winter and were valued for their powerful warming and insulating properties.

- **Kilim:** rug from the Near East and Central Asia made of cotton and goat wool and woven using a technique dating back over 10,000 years.

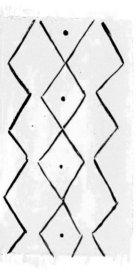

Beni Ourain

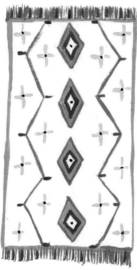

Azilal

Boujad

Boucherouite

Beni Mguild

Kilim

- AMINE BENDRIOUICH -
COUTURIER

Who are your favourite designers in Marrakesh?

Daniel Oiknine, from Métiers d'Hier: a passionate ironworker who practically lives in his workshop – he's always busy creating something. He was one of the late Pierre Bergé's favourite skilled artisans and developed several designs for him. His creations range from steampunk sculptures to industrial furniture.

Arzen is an impressive artisanal factory, founded & directed by Rachid, who has taken traditional production to new heights. When you see their brass products, you could swear they're laser cut ... but every operation is actually done by hand, in a sophisticated yet simple way that's very close to poetry.

The bag designer Zakaria Bendriouich is one of Marrakesh's most innovative artisans, skilfully melding craft, design and art. He lost a kidney in an accident, meaning that he has to drink five litres of water a day... this led to the creation of the Bido bag, literally a jerrycan bag made out of leather and upcycled plastic jerrycan parts. A whole collection followed, using the same methods and philosophy – the bags are worn by the likes of Naomi Campbell, to name just a few.

What do you reckon is the link between artisans and art?

My personal opinion might be controversial for many people, but I firmly believe that skilled craftsmanship used to be integrated with art, which in Morocco meant every aspect of life, from the utilitarian to the ornamental, from clothes to architecture, and so on. The separation between art and handicrafts occurred as a direct result of colonialism. Artisans started churning out only the designs that Wester-

ners wanted and what they thought was beautiful. The painter Jacques Majorelle was given the task of setting up the first Moroccan artisanat office, which created this false separation. Today, more and more contemporary artists are moving closer to the crafts, and more artisans are approaching their work from an artistic perspective. This will allow handicrafts to regain their original nature and status ... which is living art.

Twelve hours in Marrakesh with someone you're trying to impress?

09:30 – breakfast on the roof terrace of Shtatto, with its breathtaking views over the Medina and the entire mountain chain, then shopping in Shtatto's boutiques.

11:00 – visit to my shop. Welcome to the Kingdom.

11:30 – Moulay Youssef Lamdaghri's Bazar Coffre Mystérieux, then lunch here, prepared by Maalem Bana (this needs to be ordered one day in advance). Try Razzete Bana, his personal take on Moroccan mhancha and pastilla.

13:30 – Bazar du Sud, owned by the family who started the carpet business in Marrakesh in the 1930s as an act of resistance against the French occupation. They have some of the most unique rugs in all Morocco.

14:30 – Dar Bellarj Foundation, for whatever they're showing, from music to theatre, art and embroidery – it's generally worth the expense.

15:00 – Bert Flint Museum, one of the most splendid collections of Moroccan art.

15:45 – head out to the Medina through Riad Larousse Soui to stop at the tiny shop/atelier of Monsieur Mourtaji, one of my favourite painters in the Medina.

16:15 – Musée Farid Belkahia (Belkahia is one of the most important artists on the con-temporary Moroccan scene).

17:45 – head to Kabana, the best thing that's happened to the Medina recently. You can have a cocktail and tapas while listening to good music, with a view of the famous Koutoubia mosque and the surrounding gardens, enjoyed by lots of local people.

19:00 – dinner at Dar Simons, a fine-dining experience from a talented young Belgian chef with a subtle Moroccan influence. Delicate and fun, with a story behind every dish.

21:00 – last stop at the legendary palace of La Mamounia. Should you head for the piano retro bar or the main bar by the lobby? It's a difficult choice! But the palace was built for the prince Moulay Mamoun to enjoy nature, music and dance with his loved ones, and somehow you still get this atmosphere today, whatever you decide to do.

A GREEN OASIS
IN THE MIDDLE
OF THE MEDINA

In the heart of an old building dating from the 16th century, far from the hustle and bustle of the Medina, the Le Jardin restaurant is set in the middle of a lush garden overlooked by tastefully furnished terraces and little lounges. On the menu: a modern fusion of Moroccan and European flavours.

Kamal Laftimi's second venture (after Café des Épices), Le Jardin also serves delicious cocktails at the end of the day, so you can take full advantage of the coolness of this small urban oasis.

RESTAURANT LE JARDIN
32 SOUK JELD SIDI ABDELAZIZ

DAILY: 11am / 11pm | +212 5 24 37 82 95 | lejardinmarrakech.com

FEMINIST
COUSCOUS ACTIVISTS

Fridays are for couscous! But not just anywhere. Head to one of the centres of the association Amal, dedicated to empowering women in disadvantaged situations. Thanks to reintegration programmes, women who are divorced, widowed, single or have dependent children can develop their skills, especially in the kitchen. Have lunch here or, better still, learn to cook your favourite Moroccan dish in the company of these incredible women. Reservations are recommended.

ASSOCIATION AMAL
RUE ALLAL BEN AHMED
AND RUE IBN SINA

DAILY:
noon / 3:30pm

+212 5 24 44 68 96
amalnonprofit.org

Make reservations online for the workshops
More information on +212 5 24 49 37 76

ROOMS YOU'LL REMEMBER
FOR THE REST
OF YOUR LIFE

From romantic villas to ultra-local B&Bs, from Andalusian palaces to traditional riads, Marrakesh is teeming with an exceptional range of accommodation – you'll find some of the most incredible options outside the city.

> **The favourite retreat of aesthetes**

This retreat is set in the foothills of the mountains, in the idyllic Ourika Valley. Only 35 minutes from Marrakesh, these eco-friendly Berber lodges offer a radical change of scenery for anyone wanting to escape from the urban chaos for a bit.

© KASBAH BAB OURIKA

KASBAH BAB OURIKA
VALLÉE OURIKA, TNINE OURIKA
40 kilometers from Marrakesh

Reservations on +212 668 74 95 47	kasbahbabourika.com	From 150€ (double) to 1.650€ (private villa with swimming pool) per night Three-night minimum stay

> The rural retreat

From its hilltop, Kasbah Beldi offers an astounding view of the desert and Lalla Takerkoust Lake. Located just 50 minutes from Marrakesh, this old farm provides a breath of fresh air for anyone wishing to escape the city to spend a night under the Morrocan stars.

KASBAH BELDI
LALLA TAKERKOUST LAKE, TALET
65 kilometers from Marrakesh

+ 212 5 24 38 39 50

contact@kasbahbeldi.com
kasbahbeldi.com

© KASBAH BELDI

© LA PAUSE

> The new nomadism

Deep in the dunes of the Agafay Desert, La Pause lives up to its name. While there's no electricity or air conditioning here, what you will find is the absolute charm of a candlelit dinner and a night spent in a tent, like the nomads of old.

 LA PAUSE
DOUAR LMIH LAROUSSIENE, AGAFAY DESERT
35 kilometers from Marrakesh

Reservation on
+212 6 10 77 22 40

lapause1@gmail.com
lapause-marrakech.com

> Glamping in the dunes

Lost in the lunar landscape of the Agafay Desert, the unbleached tents of Scarabeo Camp stand out against the majestic Atlas Mountains. Sitting by a campfire, you'll feel almost like you're one of the region's first explorers.

© SCARABEO CAMP

SCARABEO CAMP
AGAFAY DESERT
35 kilometers from Marrakesh

+212 6 62 80 08 74

scarabeocamp.com
info@scarabeo-camp.com

© DAR EL SADAKA

> The unconventional riad

Designed by the artist Jean-François Fourtou, Dar el Sadaka is a truly unclassifiable villa in the heart of the Palmeraie, 20 minutes from the Medina. It's a bucolic haven where art features prominently. From the giant's house, in which all the furniture and objects are twice as big as normal, to the upside-down house with its roof resting on the ground, to rooms inhabited by animal sculptures, the entire villa invites you into an unsettling and magical universe. NB: Dar el Sadaka is only available to rent in its entirety ... Time to call a group of your best friends!

VILLA DAR EL SADAKA
8 RUE DE BAB AYLAN
10 kilometers from Marrakesh

info@darelsadaka.com
darelsadaka.com

Only available for exclusive rental,
starting from 3,400€ per night
Three-night minimum stay for up to 20 people

> A boutique hotel in the desert ▶

Driving along the small *route provinciale*, after 30 minutes, small houses made of terracotta and tadelakt come into view. This is the refuge of the Franco-Swiss architect Romain Michel-Ménière. A place of simple elegance, where the only obvious luxury is a swimming pool, ideal for cooling off on days when the scorching *sharqī* wind sweeps across the Atlas plains.

BERBER LODGE
DOUAR OUMNES, TAMESLOTH
30 kilometers from Marrakesh

+212 6 62 04 90 43	hotelberberlodge@gmail.com berberlodge.net

> The most improbable B&B in Marrakesh

This community of Gnawa musicians will give you a warm welcome in the Medina. Your days will be punctuated by guided tours (they know Marrakesh like the back of their hand), your evenings by their musical interludes … Don't let their homespun Facebook page fool you: if you're ready to live like a local in a community of artists, this is the experience for you!

GNAWA ACADEMY GUEST HOUSE
ARSET BEN CHEBI

+212 653-590031	facebook.com/Gnawa-academy-1893917984226582

BERBER LODGE

Here's a playlist to accompany you on your peregrinations around this magical city. It's a mix of Gnawa songs, minimal Eastern reveries, and traditional and contemporary sounds ... To us, it represents the aural complexity of Morocco, somewhere between musicological deep dive and electronic modernity: https://tinyurl.com/a66wt4fv

THE SOUNDS
OF MARRAKESH

Discovering Moroccan music is reason enough to travel there. Nourished by centuries of history, Islamisation, cultural exchange and intense artistic creation, the country's musical heritage is infinitely rich. Whether it's boisterous rhythms or languid rhapsodies, there's a sound to accompany every great moment in life, as well as all the little everyday things. The following is a short, non-exhaustive guide to immersing yourself in this musical odyssey.

> Once the chant of Berber shepherds, *raï* was propelled into the international arena in the 1990s by figures like Cheb Mami. Rebellious and modern, this music belongs to Morocco's youth.

> While there are many (more or less traditional) styles of *chaabi* in Morocco, it's often played at weddings and is always popular party music. The lyrics are light-hearted and the steps set to the rhythm of a *darbuka*, the goblet drum favoured by *chaabi* musicians.

> *Dakka marrakchia* is the characteristic ritual and folk music of Marrakesh, somewhere between religious incantation and African trance. Frenetic and mystical in equal measure.

> An integral part of Muslim spirituality, Sufi music is sacred. Sufi brotherhoods sometimes give concerts; otherwise, head to the Samaa Festival of Sacred Music in autumn.

> *Malhun* is sung poetry that touches on virtually every aspect and concern in the everyday life of Moroccans. A spontaneous, poetic and intergenerational art form, it has adapted perfectly to modern times. A kind of popular poetry slam.

> Widely popularised by the Gnaoua World Music Festival, which has been held in Essaouira every year since 1998, Gnaoua music has been classified as Intangible Cultural Heritage by UNESCO. On Jemaa el Fnaa square, you'll find Gnaoua musicians moving to the sound of their *guembri* (or *sintir*), the instrument they use in all their rites.

CONCOCT
THE PERFUME
OF YOUR DREAMS

In a 19th-century riad in the heart of the Medina, perfumer Abderrazzak Benchaâbane has created a space dedicated to the scents of Morocco: the Musée du Parfum (Perfume Museum).

From distillation to bottling, you'll learn everything there is to know about this delicate art as you wander through the rooms of the museum. If you're feeling daring, you can even try your hand at composing your own scent in one of the creative workshops, or have your ideal fragrance concocted at the perfume bar. The museum also organises 'olfactory awakening' workshops for children so that grown-ups can immerse themselves in their own sensory experience uninterrupted.

📍 **MUSÉE DU PARFUM**
2 DERB CHÉRIF, DIOUR SABOUN

+212 5 24 38 74 84
+212 6 61 09 53 52
+212 6 10 40 80 96

museeduparfummarrakech@gmail.com
lemuseeduparfum.com

MUSÉE DU PARFUM MARRAKECH

THE CULTURAL
OASIS

Founded in September 2013 by the brilliant Laila Hida, Le 18 is an independent platform for creation, dissemination and cultural and artistic exchange. Unique in Marrakesh and hidden in the Medina, this collective seeks to support emerging artists by offering them residencies, as well as by disseminating and exhibiting their work to the public. The perfect place to discover new talent from Marrakesh.

LE 18
18 DERB EL FERRANE, RIAD LAAROUSS

+212 5 24 38 98 64   le18marrakech@gmail.com

- LAILA HIDA -

CREATOR OF LE 18

Tell us more about your intentions when launching Le 18 – how it came to life and how it continues to thrive today.

It was intuitive, born from a desire to do and to share. The aim was to provide a creative space for other artists, researchers, curators and the general public. Le 18 evolved over time: it's similar to Moroccan houses, which usually start with two rooms, and then more rooms and living spaces are added as the family grows. In my opinion, the architecture of a cultural project should resemble this growing family whose space interacts with the need to respond to a given context.

Besides Le 18, which cultural spaces or institutions are doing a good job supporting young artists today?

Dar Bellarj, in the Medina of Marrakesh, works with a community of local women and, over time, has become an essential mediator between the young women and their families. Then there's On Marche, the yearly festival of contemporary African dance, which will host the Biennale de la Danse en Afrique (Africa Dance Biennale) in 2021. Jardin Rouge are opening their residencies to host more young local emerging artists. I must also mention L'Atelier de l'Observatoire in Casablanca; Think Tangier (based in Tangier) for their art and research residencies as well as their workshops; and the Cinémathèque de Tanger. I love the new Qisas project, which focuses on storytelling, photography and video.

These past ten years have seen a significant expansion of the cultural scene through different projects, new residencies, artists' initiatives and institutions that have emerged all over the country. The structures are still fragile but they are managing to find their own model and ecosystems.

Tell us about your favourite meal in Marrakesh!

To eat quickly and very well on a small budget, the chicken *tanjia* and *loubia* at Snack Abderrahim on Boulevard Moulay Rachid is my favourite. With a group of other people, I've also recently undertaken to compile the ultimate guide to *loubia* in Marrakesh! For a treat (also in Guéliz), try +61 for the subtlety of a mixed Australian–Mediterranean cuisine, sometimes with Asian influences – simple but exquisite. In the Medina, the most beautiful spot for lunch is Le Jardin. I simply love the place, with its greenery and very relaxed atmosphere; I can stay there for hours.

Name your three absolutely favourite spots in Marrakesh.

First, Café Imlil on Rue de la Liberté for my morning coffee and orange juice.

Second, Maison ARTC, the studio and showroom of Artsi Ifrach, a talented and fantastically creative artist. He makes everything from clothes to photography, artworks and books. His place is a great inspiration to me.

And, third, the booksellers of Bab Doukkala, where you can discover some real gems: books, old magazines, very old local journals and zines. My friend, the artist Noureddine Ezzaraf, found a whole collection of *Lamalif* (a political and cultural magazine published between 1966 and 1988) there: they are exhibited in my current show at Dar Belarj.

19

THE MUSEUM WHERE
EVERYTHING IS FOR SALE

A few steps from El Fenn, on this narrow street leading to the heart of the Medina, just before you reach the red café on your right, enter this palace from another era. Everything you see here is for sale.

In this labyrinth of antiques, you'll find centuries-old backgammon sets, improbable solid wood thrones and Judaized Berber liturgical objects dating from before the Arab conquests. A veritable Ali Baba's cave, where time seems to stand still.

TRÉSOR DES MILLE ET UNE NUITS
8 RUE EL KSOUR

+212 5 24 44 09 31

20

ONE THOUSAND AND ONE ROOFTOPS: A MAP

After wandering at length through the narrow streets of the Medina, it's a good idea to repair to higher ground at the end of the day to enjoy the sunset. Moroccan architecture is conducive to the creation of fantastic outdoor spaces, and there are countless rooftops in Marrakesh. Here is our selection of high-perched places:

> Le Shtatto

To reach Le Shtatto's superb rooftop, you have to climb three flights of stairs and go through an art gallery and several designer boutiques. From the top of this old riad, you can admire the teeming souk at the foot of the building, fresh fruit juice in hand.

 **LE SHTATTO**
81 DERB NKHAL
RAHBA LAKDIMA

DAILY: 9am / 11pm | +212 5243-75538

> L'Mida

Tucked away just a stone's throw from the Place des Épices, Omar and Simo's restaurant combines Marrakesh tradition with a taste for simple things. This Moroccan restaurant is as friendly as it is trendy and you'll relish lounging on the large green benches while waiting for your lunch.

© L'MIDA

L'MIDA
78 BIS DERB NKHEL

Reservations on +212 5 24 44 36 62   lmidamarrakech.com

> Le Kabana

Just opposite the old Koutoubia mosque, this most recent addition to the rooftop landscape has quickly established itself as the cool and cosmopolitan landmark in the Medina. You can dine here (Mediterranean cuisine and a sushi bar) or just drop in to enjoy a cocktail to the sounds of a DJ set.

LE KABANA
1 KISSARIAT BEN KHALED
RUE LALLA FATIMA EZZAHARA R'MILA

DAILY: 11am / 2am

kabana-marrakech.com

© LE KABANA

© LE CAFÉ DES ÉPICES

> Le Café des Épices

The combination of Berber cushions, low tables and views of the Atlas Mountains is pretty irresistible. This well-known little café is a not-to-be-missed spot for a pastry-and-mint-tea break in the heart of the Medina.

LE CAFÉ DES ÉPICES
75 DERB RAHBA LAKDIMA

| DAILY: 9am / 11pm | +212 5 24 39 17 70 | contact@cafedesepices.ma |
| | | cafedesepices.ma |

DIVE INTO THE KESH'S
ARTSY AND ELECTRO SIDE

Drink, Art, Food & Music is the motto of l'Envers, Marrakesh's one and only electro bar. Since its opening in 2017, party-goers have made it their headquarters, flocking here to dance to the sounds of the city's best DJs. An artsy spot par excellence, l'Envers also attracts lovers of photography and street art, who come to admire the temporary exhibitions on the walls. Others just want to meet up with friends and chill in a great atmosphere. The crowd is cosmopolitan, the cocktails well shaken, the food comforting. Go all in.

📍 **L'ENVERS**
29 RUE IBN AÏCHA, GUÉLIZ

DAILY: noon / 8pm

lenvers.ma

 # 22

THE EATERY
IN GUÉLIZ

After Café des Épices, Jardin and Nomad, the prolific Kamal Laftimi has opened another place in the heart of Guéliz. It's called Le Kilim – a tribute to the iconic Moroccan carpet.

The decor combines modernity and Moroccan tradition, as does the menu, which has the obligatory Moroccan tagines along with specialities from elsewhere, depending on the whims of chef Thomas Roger.

© LE KILIM

 LE KILIM
SIS 36 (AT THE CORNER OF TARIQ BNOU ZIAD AND RUE DE LA LIBERTÉ)

| DAILY: 7am / midnight | +212 5 24 44 69 99 | info@lekilim.com |
| | | lekilim.com |

23

ENJOY A DRINK IN
A HAVEN OF TRANQUILLITY

The beautiful Beldi Country Club not only has a souk where you can buy carpets, pottery and embroidery, but also a workshop where you can watch glassmakers in flip-flops produce Morocco's famous hand-blown glass.

While you're there, go for a stroll through the hotel's beautiful gardens and greenhouses, followed by lunch or a drink by one of the magnificent pools, where you can also take a dip. Just 20 minutes from downtown Marrakesh, the Beldi Country Club provides a particularly welcome escape from the hustle and bustle of the Medina.

© BELDI COUNTRY CLUB MARRAKECH

BELDI COUNTRY CLUB MARRAKECH
KM 6 ROUTE D'AMIZMIZ – CHRIFIA

+212 5243-83950

contact@verrebeldi.com
verrebeldi.com/fabrique

MADE IN
MARRAKESH

On the outskirts of the city, the industrial district of Sidi Gha-nem is an artisanal enclave brimming with designer workshops, trendy boutiques and showrooms of all kinds. A bustling hive where you can get your fill of inspiration strolling from interior-design shops to concept stores.

> Marrakshi Life

Since 2013, New York designer Randal Bachner has been leading the way when it comes to responsible and sustainable fashion. Imported from Egypt and Turkey, the cotton he uses is woven and dyed directly in the workshops of his brand, Marrakshi Life. Here everything is transformed and nothing is thrown away. Come visit his studio and discover all the manufacturing processes involved, from the creation of the fabric to the final product.

MARRAKSHI LIFE
933 ROUTE DE SAFI,
AL MASSAR INDUSTRIAL DISTRICT

| MON–FRI: 9am / 5pm | +212 771-613602 | marrakshilife.com |

© LRNCE STUDIO

> LRNCE Studio

You'll find nothing but beautiful things at Belgian designer Laurence Leenaert's boutique: ceramics, pillows, kimonos and leather bags inspired by Moroccan folklore and spiced up with an extremely modern graphic touch.

📍 **LRNCE STUDIO**
59 RUE SIDI GHANEM

lrnce.com
instagram.com/lrnce

> Le Magasin Général

Standing and ceiling fans, Chesterfield sofas, travel trunks ... The list of treasures available at Le Magasin Général (General Store) is seemingly never-ending. A small tour of this 'curiosity cabinet', with its faintly colonial atmosphere, is a must.

LE MAGASIN GÉNÉRAL
281 ROUTE DE SAFI,
SIDI GHANEM

MON-SAT: 10am / 6pm

magasin-general-marrakech.

> Unum

Unum is a haven for small designers. This multifaceted concept store is filled with unique and original objects, from ready-to-wear clothing and beautiful tea sets to perfumes. A perfect place to shop.

UNUM
366 SIDI GHANEM

MON-FRI: 10am / 6pm
SAT: 10am / 1pm

unumcreation.com

> Galerie Pop

In a large white loft, Galerie Pop brings together Moroccan and foreign designers, artisans, retailers and artists. Halfway between a showroom and an art gallery, this artsy cave is packed with accessories, ceramics and designer furniture.

GALERIE POP
109-4 AVENUE PRINCIPALE,
SIDI GHANEM

MON-FRI: 10am / 6pm
SAT: 10am / 2pm

+212 5243-36008

© SOME

> Some

Here's a concept store that meets the challenge of being super local but also supremely elegant. For a little over three years, this boutique villa located in the heart of the Guéliz district has been working in close collaboration with skilled Moroccan artisans. You'll find accessories, decorative objects and recyclable unfinished furniture (you can choose all the finishes). Don't forget to have a coffee in the garden before you leave.

SOME
76 BOULEVARD MANSOUR EDHABI

| TUE-SAT: 10am / 6pm | +212 5244-33372 | someslowconcept.com |

- AMINE KABBAJ -

ARCHITECT, PRESIDENT OF THE MARRAKECH BIENNALE
FOR CONTEMPORARY ART

You talk a lot about the context in which Marrakesh exists and without which it's impossible to fully grasp the city's historical importance. Which historical places define it?

The problem for me is that Marrakesh can't be defined by its centre alone. Marrakesh is also what's around this core. This is important because if you consider only the Medina, you disconnect yourself from its history. Marrakesh only makes sense within its context – and that context is the Atlas Mountains; Marrakesh was born from the Atlas Mountains. The first capital (before Marrakesh) was Aghmat, located 35 km to the south. Starting from there, the following sites are must-sees: the Yagour plateau and its rock carvings (a journey back in time to

5000 BC); the Great Mosque of Tinmel (the foundation of the largest Moroccan empire under the Almohads); Aghmat (the birth of the Almoravids and their conquest of Spain); the Oued Tensift bridge (an often ignored work of art built by the Almoravids over 900 years ago); the Agdal and Menara Gardens, with their water reservoirs for the olive groves; the Walls of Marrakesh; the Jbel Guéliz; the dry Oued Issil river, which divides Marrakesh from east to west; the Almoravid Qubba; the Koutoubia mosque; Dar el Bacha Palace, the residence of notables; Bahia Palace; Dar Si Said; El Badi Palace (a royal residence that rivals Versailles); the fountains where animals and humans drank; the Mellah (Jewish quarter);

and the Saadian Tombs, a protected necropolis.

Which novels do you think best sum up the history of Morocco and Marrakesh?

Jacques Attali's *La confrérie des éveillés* (Brotherhood of the Awakened) and Gilbert Sinoué's *Averroès ou le secrétaire du diable* (Averroès or The Devil's Secretary). Ibn Tufail is also a must-read – he was the mentor of Ibn Rushd (or Averroës), who wrote in the late 12th century and inspired the character of Robinson Crusoe. I also strongly recommend the work of Nabil Mouline, an eminent young Moroccan historian, and of Ahmed Toufiq, Minister for Islamic Affairs, who is an excellent novelist and has written extensively on the history of Morocco.

AMINE KABBAJ'S GUIDE TO THE MEDINA

- **Belhaj**: for jewellery and traditional silver objects; next to Bab Ftouh and the Foundouk Ouarzazi Souk.

- **Chez Jilali**: a fantastic flea market, right next to the dyers. Belhaj and Jilali are two of the most traditional, authentic people.

- **Marché Subsaharien**: for beautiful sub-Saharan African fabrics, indigo and Ivorian and Senegalese textiles

- **Abdelsakt Ouzid**: another quality flea market, next to the Mouassine mosque.

- **L'Atrach**: a recent silverware business. Items also sold by La Mamounia.

- **Soumia Kabbaj**: for traditional clothing.

- **Fatim Zahra bel Attar**: for dates, raisins, peanuts, etc.

- **Mishi**: a fun Japanese–Moroccan shop for unique clothing and objects. Moroccan handicrafts with a Japanese twist.

- **Hamid**: for authentic babouche slippers!

- **Khalid Art Gallery**: the Medina's luxury second-hand dealer, with five or six shops between the Medina and the Yves Saint Laurent Museum.

- **Pikala**: a very well-known and respected association in the Medina, founded by a Dutch woman. They offer training to young people in Marrakesh as professional bicycle tour guides; the bikes are just an excuse for discovering the city, a way to see it from a different perspective.

THE TREASURES OF
MOULAY YOUSSEF

Moulay Youssef is well known among Moroccan antique lovers beyond the gates of Marrakesh. Second-hand aficionados are forever wanting to emulate this key dealer's finds. Anyone looking to furnish their home owes it to themselves to rummage through his sensational bric-a-brac.

SHOP MOULAY YOUSSEF
RUE FERKLA

+212 6 68 94 81 15

THE BEST
ORANGE JUICE
ON JEMAA EL FNAA

It's impossible to leave Jemaa el Fnaa square without some freshly squeezed juice from one of the street vendors. If you can manage to evade the snake charmers and babouche sellers, head over to stand 26, our favourite.

Ask for your orange juice without any added sugar or water. Sublime. If you start to feel peckish, head straight to a fried-fish stand or, better still, a grill – the best ones on the square are right next door!

PLACE DJEMAA EL FNA
STAND 26

DAILY: 9am / midnight

THE 'PICASSO'
OF THE MEDINA

In the cramped but very busy studio of this elderly Marrakesh painter, Monsieur Mourtaji, you'll find portraits of every king who has ruled Morocco, but also of icons such as our old friend, the Mona Lisa ... Slightly surreal, naive and touching, Mourtaji's works are known throughout the Medina.

Come and visit this little shop devoted to painting ... on canvas, on teapots and on anything that a paintbrush can embellish.

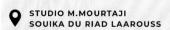

STUDIO M.MOURTAJI
SOUIKA DU RIAD LAAROUSS

A CULINARY
WORLD TOUR

If, after a few days, you can't bear the thought of even one more grain of couscous, this selection of spots is for you. Six places offering a delicious and uncompromising break, with Australian, Lebanese and vegetarian fare on the menu.

> **Azar**

Hummus, falafel, kibbeh, tzatziki ... When you go to Azar, it's because you're hankering for an excellent Lebanese alternative. Warmed by the scent of shisha smoke, the atmosphere is hushed, until oriental dancers liven things up at 10 pm. Let yourself be buoyed up too.

AZAR
RUE DE YOUGOSLAVIE
(ON THE SIDE OF BOULEVARD HASSAN II),
GUÉLIZ

DAILY: from 7pm · +212 5244-30920 · contact@azar-marrakech.com
azarmarrakech.com

© ROYAL MANSOUR

> ### Sesamo

Walking through the door of the sumptuous restaurant Sesamo promises to teleport you instantly to the wonderful world of Italian gastronomy. Try the spicy pesto risotto or the famous squid cappuccino. As exquisite as it is expensive.

📍 **SESAMO**
ROYAL MANSOUR
EL SEBTI, RUE ABOU AL ABBAS

| DAILY: noon / 3:30pm 7pm / 10pm | +212 5248-08282 | restauration@royalmansour.ma royalmansour.com/en/dining/ sesamo-marrakesh |

> Le Gaïa

Juice bar, delicatessen, tea room and craft shop – this charming vegetarian restaurant effortlessly wears all these hats. The food is colourful, fresh and organic, the prices more than fair.

LE GAÏA
100 RUE MOHAMMED EL BEQAL

| MON–SAT:
noon / 7:30pm | +212 770 207030 | gaia-vegetarian-restaurant.business.site |

© LE GAÏA

© +61

> ## Le +61

Simple, generous and relaxed, chef Andrew Cibej's cuisine consists of the best of Australian gastronomy. No fuss, all flavour.

+61
96 RUE MOHAMMED EL BEQAL

Dh Dh

WED-SAT: noon / 8pm   plus61.com

> Le Mandala

Le Mandala is a family affair and a love story between Moroccan and Scandinavian cuisine. An improbable culinary union that brings the best of both cultures, from 100% Arabica coffees to divinely smoked fish.

MANDALA
159 RUE RIAD ZITOUN EL JDID

+212 80 8534712   mandalamaroc.com

© MANDALA

> La Famille

What a delight to have lunch in the shade of the bougainvillea in La Famille's garden! Vegetarian, organic and ultra-fresh, the menu at this small, highly Instagrammable spot changes daily according to what's available at the market. And the temptations don't end there: there's also a boutique corner with a lovely selection of objects and jewellery by Stephanie Jewels.

© LA FAMILLE

LA FAMILLE
42 RUE RIAD ZITOUN EL JDID,
(NEXT TO THE BAHIA PALACE)

Dh Dh

| MON–SAT: noon / 4pm | Reservations required on +212 5243-85295 | instagram.com/la_famille_marrakech |

SPICES
ON THE ROCKS

The huge iron 'B' hides a small staircase leading to one of the trendiest places in Guéliz: Le Baromètre. With its decor reminiscent of an early 20th-century American speakeasy, Morocco's first mixology bar will intoxicate you with its retro atmosphere and incredible cocktails.

Leaning on the counter, you can watch the drink you've ordered being made, step by step, subtly enhanced with spices, aromatic herbs, floral waters and macerated fruits.

An exotic liquid garden of sorts that you can sip in a very New York atmosphere.

BAR LE BAROMÈTRE
RUE MOULAY ALI

| MON–SAT: 6:30pm / 11pm | +212 5243-79012 | To register for mixology courses and for more info: inforesa@lebarometre.net |

WILD ABOUT
GREASY SPOONS

You can't judge a country's culinary culture without trying its greasy spoons. They're legion in Marrakesh. These are our favourites (forget what they look like from the outside; you'll just have to trust us on this).

> Chez Bejgueni

Hands down, one of the best places for grilled lamb chops. Tourists are welcomed like locals here, with straightforward and friendly service.
21 rue Ibn Aïcha, Guéliz
Daily: 10am / 10pm

> Chez Ouazzani

Meat lovers shouldn't miss this small restaurant in Guéliz. The dishes are hearty and bursting with flavour, the prices decidedly affordable.
12 bis rue Ibn Aïcha, Guéliz
Daily: noon / 2am

> Al Bahriya

Marrakesh natives have been licking their fingers in delight at this little seafood eatery for almost 30 years. Choose what you want from the large stand and it will be sent over to the plancha before finally landing on your plate.
75 boulevard Moulay Rachid
Daily: 11:45am / 1am

We never reveal the 31st address in the 'Soul of' series
because it's strictly confidential.
Up to you to find it!

MOHAMED BARIZ,
THE VOICE OF MOROCCO

Once upon a time, there was Mohamed Bariz, who told his country's most beautiful stories. When he was just 12 years old, he was already captivating passers-by on Jemaa el Fnaa square, keeping alive an art that barely survives in Morocco today. Forty years later, he still performs in Arabic, French and English at festivals around the world as one of the last representatives of this ancient tradition of itinerant storytelling. He's fighting body and soul to save this fragile art, and the best way you can support him in this struggle is by listening to him and allowing him to remind you of your childhood dreams.

 To meet this unique soul, ask around at the stalls on Jemaa el Fnaa square; the orange-juice sellers might let you know where you can find him …

Tales in Arabic, French and English

AKNOWLEDGEMENTS

Fabrice would like to thank:

ZOHAR for having shared *his* Marrakesh with me and for the beautiful moments of laughter and friendship experienced there.

LUCIE for her invaluable help with the texts, her unflagging good mood and for dealing with my eternal geographic and scheduling confusion.

OKSANA for having spent many hours gathering a great deal of valuable practical information.

ALL OUR MARRAKSHI FRIENDS for their generosity, openness, willingness to share and ability to reveal this city in all its richness and complexity.

Zohar would like to thank:

FABRICE for bringing me in to this project and allowing me to rediscover a city that's so close to my heart and soul.

ABDELAALI AIT KARROUM, our photographer, for his patience and for continually finding creative ways to shoot a city in the midst of a pandemic.

ANNAELLE MYRIAM CHAAIB, (aka Myriam au citron), our talented illustrator, for her courage and for bringing colour and warmth to this book with her 'naïf'-style depictions of Marrakesh.

MY MOTHER, THE SLAOUI FAMILY, AMINE KABBAJ AND AMINE BENDRIOUICH for holding my hand through the proverbial secret alleyways of Marrakesh and astonishing me each time with new discoveries that delight the eye and new encounters that renew your faith in the magic of travel.

This book was created by:
Fabrice Nadjari and Zohar Benjelloun, authors
Abdelaali Ait Karroum, photos
Annaelle Myriam Chaaib, illustrations
Emmanuelle Willard Toulemonde, layout
Sophie Schlondorff, translation
Jana Gough, copy-editing
Kimberly Bess, proofreading
Clémence Mathé, publishing

You can write to us at contact@soul-of-cities.com
Follow us on Instagram on @soul_of_guides

THANK YOU

In the same collection:

Soul of Athens

Soul of Barcelona

Soul of Kyoto

Soul of Lisbon

Soul of Los Angeles

Soul of New York

Soul of Roma

Soul of Tokyo

Soul of Venice

In accordance with regularly upheld French jurisprudence (Toulouse 14-01-1887), the publisher will not be deemed responsible for any involuntary errors or omissions that may subsist in this guide despite our diligence and verifications by the editorial staff.

Any reproduction of the content, or part of the content, of this book by whatever means is forbidden without prior authorization by the publisher.

© JONGLEZ 2022

Registration of copyright: January 2022 – Edition: 01

ISBN: 978-2-36195-465-9

Printed in Slovakia by Polygraf